THE
SPHINX

MONSTERS OF MYTHOLOGY

25 VOLUMES

Hellenic

Amycus
Anteus
The Calydonian Boar
Cerberus
Chimaera
The Cyclopes
The Dragon of Boeotia
The Furies
Geryon
Harpalyce
Hecate
The Hydra
Ladon
Medusa
The Minotaur
The Nemean Lion
Procrustes
Scylla and Charybdis
The Sirens
The Spear-birds
The Sphinx

Norse

Fafnir
Fenris

Celtic

Drabne of Dole
Pig's Ploughman

MONSTERS OF MYTHOLOGY

THE
SPHINX

Bernard Evslin

CHELSEA HOUSE PUBLISHERS

New York   Philadelphia

1991

EDITOR
Remmel Nunn

ART DIRECTOR
Maria Epes

PICTURE RESEARCHERS
Susan Quist, Georganne M. Backman

SENIOR DESIGNER
Marjorie Zaum

EDITORIAL ASSISTANTS
Seeta Chaganti, Nate Eaton, Mark Rifkin

5 7 9 8 6

Library of Congress Cataloging-in-Publication Data

Evslin, Bernard.
The Sphinx/Bud Evslin.

p. cm.—(Monsters of mythology.)
Summary: Recounts the myth of the Sphinx, a monster with a lion's
body, an eagle's wings, and a woman's head.
ISBN 1-55546-260-X
1. Sphinxes (Mythology)—Juvenile literature. [1. Sphinxes
(Mythology) 2. Mythology, Greek.] I. Title. II. Series:
Evslin, Bernard.
Monsters of mythology.
BL820.S66E97   1990   398.21—dc20
89-77769   CIP   AC

Printed and bound in Mexico.

In that ancient lovely tongue, Dorothy means
gift of the Goddess. And I thank her.

Contents

Characters

Monsters

The Sphinx (SFINKS)	Atrocious monster with lion's body, eagle's wings, and woman's head
Harpies	Flying hags who police Hell
Giants	Hundred-handed creatures who serve Zeus and Hades
Cyclopes (SY kloh peez)	Gigantic one-eyed smiths
Cerberus (SER beh ruhs)	Three-headed dog who guards the Gates of Hell

Gods

Zeus (ZOOS)	King of the Gods
Hades (HAY deez)	Lord of Tartarus, the Land Beyond Death
Demeter (DEM ih tuhr)	Goddess of the Harvest
Persephone (per SEF uh nee)	Demeter's daughter, the spring goddess

Poseidon (poh SY duhn)	God of the Sea
Hermes (HUR meez)	The Messenger God, Usher of the Dead
Hera (HEE ruh)	Wife to Zeus; Queen of the Gods

Mortals

Thallo	A poet
Charon (KAH ron)	Master boatman who ferries shades across the Styx
Oedipus (ED ih puhs)	King of Thebes

Others

Menthe (MEN thee)	Meadow nymph who serves Demeter
Griffin	Winged lion that fathered the Sphinx
Lila	Desert demon who bore the Sphinx
Serpents	They prowl Tartarus
Fiends and Demons	Employed by Hades to administer torments
Wingless Dragons	Specially bred to serve in Hell
Thanatos (THAN ah tohs)	Diplomatic demon, Hades' chief of staff

1

Enter the Sphinx

n a desert, long ago, dwelt a tribe of female demons who rode sandstorms and raided caravans. They lived in what is now north India, and had made themselves feared by everyone. Until, one night, their "queen was stepped on by an elephant. Too tough to die, she was too squashed to rule, and passed the crown on to her daughter, the princess Lila. And Lila, made reckless by joy, gathered the tribe about her and said:

"Hear me now. We are grown false to ourselves through easy living. For some time now our only forays have been against caravanning merchants who are unable to put up a decent fight. So we scatter them, help ourselves to their gold and their jewelry, and roast their camels, and a few of the fattest merchants—and count our booty and sleep, and are visited by no dreams of glory. We are not meant for so soft a life, swift sisters. We are lean and mean and keen. Aye, we twirl the sand into whirling spouts and spin in the midst of them in a fine demon dance. And all who dwell in this dry land dread our name. So . . . let us use our powers lest they wither and fall away. Let us raid a truly worthy foe."

"Who . . . who?" screeched the coven.

"Why, the Griffins."

"No! No! Woe! Woe!" the witches shrieked in dismay. Although they were savage in battle, they had no stomach for fighting Griffins—and with good reason.

For these creatures were winged lions, but their heads were eagle heads. When hunting they darkened the sky, then dived like eagles falling upon a flock of sheep. But what they ate were elephants, hippos, camels, and gorillas. And there were strong rumors that they spent their time when not hunting in scratching gold out of the desert sand—and had heaped up a mountain of gold.

"Don't say 'no,' " said Lila. "Don't say 'woe.' Anyone who denies my leadership must meet me in single combat."

She stood to her full, towering height and stretched her powerful arms. And no one dared challenge her, much as they feared the Griffins. For she was the largest of them by far, and wrestled crocodiles for sport.

That night, under the indifferent gaze of the great low desert stars, they whirled in a demon dance. Raised cones and funnels of sand that enclosed each one in a fine, suffocating grip. Whirling, dancing, shrieking, they moved across the desert to where the Griffins dwelt.

All night they traveled, and through the morning hours, and then at noon, when the sand was as hot as iron filings, they struck. They fell upon the Griffins in a stifling rush. But the winged lions were swifter still. Beating their eagle vans, they rose into the air, then fell with bared claws.

What happened then exactly was hidden in spouts of sand and gouts of blood. And the story itself of that strange battle has blown away like desert dust. What we do know is this: A few witches managed to escape; the rest were torn to shreds. Except for Lila: she was taken captive by the Griffin chief. And when he released her she did not wish to go, but dwelt with him for many centuries.

She presented him with a daughter, it is said. And that

daughter had a woman's head, a lion's body, and an eagle's wings. They named her Sphinx, and she grew to Griffin size in a single day. She stayed with the Griffins for a week or so, then decided that she preferred to hunt alone. So she left her mother and father and the Griffin pack, and flew far away.

The Sphinx developed extreme tastes. She either craved or loathed, nothing between. She loved intense heat and hated the cold. The place she was fondest of was the very middle of the Egyptian desert where the sand under the midday sun grew hot as molten gold. And there is where she would have dwelt always had it not been so hard to find food.

For she had a very picky appetite. Her favorite meal was a kind of humpbacked whale that sang as it swam, and even sang on its way down her gullet, tickling her palate in a very pleasurable way. Among land animals she preferred a certain silvery ape. And these preferences made her bad temper worse. For the whales soon learned how much the Sphinx hated to be cold, and began to hide in the deepest gulches of the sea where the water was icy. By the time the Sphinx caught a whale, she would have to fly off to the desert and burrow under the sand and stay there until she thawed. So, finally, she gave up on the singing whales and began to hunt giant octopi and two-ton sea turtles—which filled her belly but gave her no pleasure.

As for the silvery ape, it was considered a delicacy also by lions and tigers and leopards and such, and its numbers were shrinking fast. So the Sphinx had to eat gorillas and baboons— who were nourishing but flavorless.

She found herself feeding, therefore, less heavily than she liked, and felt always half-starved. And her temper grew worse and worse.

2

An Unlikely Match

hen Hecate announced that she meant to wed the lame little poet, Thallo, no one could understand why. But the assorted fiends and demons who staffed Hell had learned not to question the tigerishly beautiful Harpy queen no matter what she did. In the vast realm of the Land Beyond Death only Hades, its king, claimed authority over her, and he didn't trust himself to approach her. The idea that his chief aide should wish to leave his employ threw him into such a fury that he kept his distance. He knew that if he came close he would assault her—and even he didn't relish closing with that savage creature. For her great wings bore her more swiftly than an eagle, and her brass talons could rip an armored giant to shreds.

No one questioned her, therefore, when she quit Tartarus forever and flew off to Helicon to collect her unsuspecting man.

The rabble of poets who were wandering the slope of Parnassus, picking flowers and muttering bits of verse to themselves, scattered like quail when a huge, winged shadow fell upon them. Thallo alone did not flee, but sat on his rock, grinning, as Hecate alighted.

"A good day to you," he said.

Thallo alone did not flee,
but sat on his rock.

"A very good one," she said. "My wedding day."

"Oh, are you to be married?"

"Yes."

"To whom?"

"To you, of course."

"Me? Why me?"

"That's either a modest answer or an extremely rude one. And I hope for your sake that it's not rude."

"Let's put it this way," he drawled. "We've had a few

sprightly conversations, and I'm aware of a kind of excitement between us, but a man does expect to be courted, you know.''

"Everyone else is shocked by my choice," she said. "So you may as well be too. While I make it a rule never to explain myself, I will say this: I have certain powers and have gained a certain measure of fame, but now I intend to devote myself entirely to you.''

"Thank you," said Thallo. "You are the Arch Tormentress, are you not?''

"So I have been called," she said modestly.

"And now you wish to focus these impressive talents upon me?''

"On you alone, sweetling.''

"Wish to quit public service and contrive a little private hell for me, is that it?''

"You have a way with words, gimpy one," she murmured. "That's how you won my heart.''

She unsheathed her brass claws and raked him tenderly. He shuddered with delight.

Her claws closed upon him; her wings beat the air; they arose. He dangled from her claws, laughing, still clutching the thick scroll on which was written the tale he had been working on for the past twenty years. He used it now to wave good-bye to his fellow poets, who were staring up in amazement.

3

The Ferryman

hessaly is studded with mountains. For three months of the year they are clad in snow. But spring comes early there, and the melted snow cascades down to flood the rivers.

Of all these swift-flowing rivers the most perilous was Alpheus. Centuries before, an idle, mischievous river god by the same name fell in love with a nymph named Arethusa. He pursued her over the field and through the wood and was about to catch her when she gained the aid of Artemis, who changed her into a stream. Whereupon Alpheus changed himself into a river and sought to mingle his waters with the stream. But Artemis dammed him up and left him in thwarted flood. This curdled his disposition, which was not too good to begin with. He boiled with spiteful currents and tried to drown anyone crossing him. He also delighted in overflowing his banks, washing away towns and farms and drowning cattle.

Now, in the beginning of things man had not yet learned bridge building. The only way to cross a swift river was by boat, and this was dangerous also. To be a ferryman demanded great strength and courage. And the one who ferried folk across the treacherous Alpheus was the most experienced boatman in Thessaly, a gigantic grizzled old fellow named Abas. He had worked the river for more than fifty years, and seemed as powerful as ever. But he wasn't quite. Suddenly one fair summer day the river went into spate. Abas was swept overboard and drowned.

His place was immediately taken, to everyone's surprise, by his eighteen-year-old son, named Charon. Nobody objected, however, when the young man claimed his father's post. For he was a hulking youth, much too big for anyone to challenge.

In order to carry more passengers, Charon decided to use a raft instead of a boat. He made it himself, felling a massive oak, trimming it, chopping it into logs, and binding them with vines.

He was a hulking youth,
much too big for anyone to challenge.

For an oar he used the trimmed trunk of a smaller tree. When he finished he had a huge, heavy, clumsy thing, more of a floating platform than a vessel. But he was so powerful that he sent it scudding across the river like a canoe.

The silent youth and his giant raft became very popular. After a month or so, more people were traveling with him than had ever crossed with his father.

One day, however, things were slow, and it was hours before a single passenger came to the dock. Charon eyed him closely, not liking what he saw—a big, burly fellow with a greasy beard. He wore a leather tunic and bore a heavy knobbed club. But he smiled at Charon and wished him good day.

Charon grunted, and said, "Get aboard."

"I don't want to cross," said the man.

"What do you want then?"

"Just to talk to you."

"Talk?"

"Is that so strange?"

"You'll have to talk on board. There may be people on the far shore waiting to be picked up."

The stranger stepped onto the raft. Charon dipped his oar and with a mighty thrust sent the clumsy craft scudding along.

"You handle this thing well," said the stranger. "And I know. I'm a ferryman myself."

Charon said nothing.

"In fact, I'm chief of the clan."

"What clan?" Charon grunted.

"Ferrymen."

"That's no clan; it's an occupation."

"Well, this is what I want to talk to you about. All the other ferrymen have joined up. You're the only one who isn't a member."

"And I don't mean to be."

"Why not?"

"I don't want to cross," said the man.

"Why yes?"

"We do each other a lot of good. Help each other."

"How?"

"Fix fares."

"How do you mean?"

"Well, before we got together, people paid us anything they felt like. A small coin, a sack of apples, a sausage. And those who had nothing gave nothing."

"So . . . ?"

"It's no good. We had a meeting and decided to raise fares—and in such a way that our passengers couldn't object; that's the beauty part. What we do is simply stop the boat in the middle of the river and tell them to empty their pockets."

"Suppose they don't?"

"We reason with them for a minute or two, and if they're still stubborn we hit them on the head with an oar and toss them overboard. Works like a charm. None of us had to drown more than one or two before people saw the light. Now, we're doing very well."

"If you're doing so well, why are you bothering with me?"

"Because if even one ferryman does things in the old way it makes the rest of us look bad. In fact, we've noticed that people are going out of their way to cross over with you instead of using the river nearest them."

"I'm not surprised," said Charon.

"What it amounts to, brother, is that we'll have to insist that you join up."

"Insist how?"

"Well, if you don't see reason and enroll yourself in the clan and start fleecing your riders like a good loyal member, then we'll have to take drastic measures."

"Drastic, eh?"

"I'm afraid so."

"Want my answer now?"

"Yes."

Charon stopped rowing. Unshipped his oar, raised it high and smashed it down on the man's head. He caught the slumping body, whisked it into the air, and pitched it into the river—where it sank immediately. He dipped his oar, and with a powerful stroke drove the raft toward the other shore.

4

Menthe

or some months now Alpheus had been fast asleep under the river that bore his name. Then in the first week of spring he awoke, hungry and irritable—in a mood for drowning people. But there were no fishermen on the banks, no swimmers on the rocks, and he knew that he would have to wait until someone boarded the ferry.

But no one came to the old wooden dock. The raft was moored, and Charon lounged on it, braiding a rope. Alpheus squatted underwater, watching the shadows that slid across the surface. He glared at the shadow of the raft. He disliked everyone, but had formed a special distaste for the big, raw youth who plied his river so boldly.

"I'd drown him now," thought Alpheus, "but I want to wait until he has some passengers."

Upon that early spring day Charon was in a strange mood also. The wind blowing off the mountain was heavy with fragrance. Odor of clover and hot meadow grass mingled with the cool smell of mountain trees—cedar and pine. And the warm wind was striped with a colder air—a whiff of the last snow clinging to the crags. It was a maddening incense. Charon drew great draughts of it into the bellows of his chest. Then it seemed that fragrance became song as the birds welcomed the day; meadowlark and blackbird and the silver-noted throstle.

Charon felt himself boiling with restlessness, the kind that could not be drained off by terrific labors. Using his muscles was not enough upon this day; he wanted to use more of himself. But what more was there? The question burned in him. To cool himself off he jumped into the river, and was seized by a strong undertow—something he had not known since he had begun working as a ferryman. It was sucking him under.

Snorting, he broached like a dolphin, arching up out of the water. When he fell back he was again clutched by the undertow, which had grown stronger. He was delighted to be fighting something. The thews of his back and upper arms writhed like serpents under his bronze skin as he cleaved the water with powerful strokes. He drew himself onto the wharf.

"Bravo!" said a thin voice. "You're a marvelous swimmer."

"Marvelous!" piped another voice. "A pleasure to watch you."

Charon brushed the water from his eyes and saw two little people, very ancient, either twins or husband and wife who had grown to look exactly like each other—except for the long white beard worn by the man.

Charon pointed to the raft and across the river.

"Yes," said the wife. "We'd like to cross, please."

"What's the fare?" asked the man.

Charon shrugged.

The woman unpinned a brooch from her tunic, her only ornament; it was made of bronze, with a tiny blue stone. Charon shook his head and motioned her to pin it back on. She smiled and fished into a small sack she was carrying. She took out a loaf of bread.

"New baked," she said. "And delicious, if I say so myself."

The man nodded and smiled greedily to show how good he knew it to be.

Charon took the bread, broke off half a loaf, and stuffed it into his mouth. He tore the rest of it in two and gave a piece to each of the old couple. They had no teeth but their gums seemed very tough, and they mumbled the bread hungrily as Charon helped them onto the raft and began rowing toward the far shore.

Then, Alpheus struck.

He hunched his mighty shoulders, twisting the river currents into a single taut sinew of water that slid under the raft and flipped it over. Alpheus chortled and spun about, churning the river into a gigantic whirlpool. The old folk were sucked under. Charon was swimming toward them as fast as he could when he saw them disappear.

Without hesitation, he dived after them. He was in a whirling funnel of water. He felt himself being spun violently, his head knocking against his knees. The brutal force behind the water made it seem solid, not liquid. Battered as Charon was, he kept churning his way toward where he saw the old man and old woman sinking, hands clasped. The thought that they loved each other so much that they couldn't bear to be parted, even in death, filled him with a rage of pity—which turned into strength and allowed him to cleave the water toward them.

He reached them, tucked them under one arm, and kicked his way to the surface.

Alpheus couldn't believe he hadn't drowned them. He seized the three of them in a gigantic watery hand and swept them toward a rock. They were going with such speed that Charon knew that they would be crushed to a pulp against the boulder. Trying to slow himself, he sank under, drawing a huge breath before he submerged, holding one arm above the surface so that the old folk could cling to it.

He curled his legs as he went, and as soon as he felt his feet touch the rock, he uncoiled, exerting all his strength in one last desperate leap. He shot out of the water.

Still clutching the man and woman, he curved in the air and landed on the shore.

Alpheus hurled water after them, a heavy sheet of it, curling like an ocean breaker, but Charon jumped away, bearing the old couple far enough inland to be safe from the boiling river.

But when he set them gently on the grass, they felt like a bundle of wet rags, and he feared that, despite all his efforts, Alpheus had succeeded in drowning them.

Out of the rags sprouted a form. Charon gasped. It was not the old woman rising, but taller than her, taller than a young woman, taller than a man. A nymph. A meadow nymph with a mane of glossy chestnut hair and leaf-green eyes. She smiled at him and he felt the heat rising in his huge body, squeezing his windpipe, pressing his eyeballs.

He looked her up and down. Her bare feet spurned the rags. Her long, bronzed body gleamed with wetness. She cast a fragrance of sunshine and crushed mint. She seemed to be swaying closer without moving. For the first time in his life he felt himself trembling.

"Who are you?" he muttered.

"I am Menthe."

"And the old woman?"

"What about her?"

"Who was she? Where is she?"

"Nowhere now. She was just a disguise."

"And the old man?"

"Nowhere too. Part of the costume, you know."

"I don't know. Tell me: Why all this bother? Who were you trying to fool?"

"Enemies."

"Who would try to harm you?"

"Those who try to harm my mistress. I serve a goddess who is feuding with someone even mightier than herself. She was afraid he would learn about my mission and send his creatures to catch me before I could get where I was going. Therefore did I travel as that feeble old couple you were so kind to."

"And this form I see before me now—is this another disguise?"

"No. It is me, myself, as I am."

"An improvement," grunted Charon. "So have you gotten to where you're going?"

"I have. Right here. It is you I have come to see."

"But why?"

"My mistress needs your assistance."

"Didn't you say she was a goddess?"

"I did."

"Which one?"

"Demeter. The Barley Mother. Lady of the Harvest. Mistress of Growing Things."

"Why should such a one need the help of a mere ferryman?"

"I don't know. But she says she does. It is not for me to question her."

"But it's for me if she wants me to do something for her."

"Indeed, yes. But she will tell you herself. We must go to her."

"Where is she?"

"Eleusis."

"A long journey."

She smiled at him. "We shall travel together."

"I'm ready."

5

The Barley Mother

hey passed through an empty landscape. No one was working the fields. No one was visible about the occasional farm hut, save one chained dog howling miserably. Charon thought that the people must have flocked to the village upon this day for some celebration. But when they came to the village, it too was empty; not even a dog to be seen.

Then, as they passed through the village into the fields again, Charon heard a seething murmur that grew louder and louder as they walked. It sounded like the surf battering cliffs, but they were far from the sea.

And then he saw where the people had gone. They were thronging a huge plain; in the middle of this plain sat a low hill. The people did not stand. Men, women, and children were crouched upon the ground, some kneeling, as if in worship, or fear, or both.

Now Charon saw what had brought them there and was pressing them to the ground. On the hill towered something tall— so tall that at first he mistook it for a tree. But as he walked through the kneeling people and came closer to the hill, he saw that it was an enormous female figure clad in flowing robes. Upon her head was a braided crown of flowers. She was shaking her long white arms, now roaring at the crowd, now seeming to scold the skies.

"Hunger will stalk the land," she cried. "No seed shall sprout, no furrow quicken. Barren shall be the fields, the orchards blasted and fruitless. And the cattle, unable to graze, shall starve, and the herdsmen and the plowmen, and their families also. For I, Demeter, Bestower of Crops, am angry, furiously angry, and my wrath is famine. Until high justice is done, until Zeus reverses his decision and declares in my favor, and bids the foul abductor return my daughter to her mother's arms, then all the land shall share my grief."

As the goddess was pronouncing these terrible words Charon and Menthe were threading their way toward her. Finally they could go no farther. The crowd was denser near the hill— a stiff, resistant hedge of crouched bodies. Charon saw that the green-clad one was beckoning to him and knew that he would have to go to her. To do so, though, he would have to brutally trample a path through the mob. His neck swelled with cruel energy—like that of a bull about to charge.

Menthe put her hand on his neck, and he felt a coolness wash through his hot, throbbing body. "Wait," she murmured. She raised her arm.

A huge white goat appeared between them, and stood there like a pillar of white fire. Its horns were golden in the slant afternoon sun; its eyes were amber slits of light. Menthe floated onto the goat's back and grasped its horns. Charon pulled himself up after her. The goat leaped. A gigantic leap. It soared over the crowd and landed on the hill—knelt to the goddess so that Menthe and Charon slid off and stood before her.

Charon was enveloped in her fragrance. She smelled like ploughed fields after a light rain. Her voice wrapped about him also; it was like the wind among trees.

"Thank you," she said. "I have sent for you, and you have come."

Charon heard himself speaking words he hadn't thought of. "How may I serve you?"

"I need your help to save my daughter from her foul abductor."

"He must be powerful as well as foul," said Charon, "if someone like you needs help to reclaim her own."

"He is Hades, Lord of the Underworld, my eldest brother, and brother to Zeus too, of course. You heard me pronounce his name to these poor starvelings, did you not?"

"I was too busy trying to get through the crowd to attend to what you were saying. But I understand now. Hades has taken your girl. I don't know her name."

"Persephone, the April Child, Maiden of the Changing Year. Just five days ago she was in the meadow with her paint box coloring the wildflowers, when the earth cracked and out charged a black chariot drawn by six black stallions. The charioteer was my accursed brother. He snatched her up from among her flowers, wrapped her in his cloak, drank her tears, and whipped the stallions back into the pit . . . down into his damned realm—into Tartarus itself. And there he keeps her, and defies me to take her back."

"And you have sought justice from Zeus—is that what I heard you tell the multitude?"

"Aye, and you heard me say that justice was denied. Certainly I rushed up to Olympus, confronted Zeus in the Hall of Judgment. There he sat on his golden throne in his cloak patterned with stars, and listened silently as I poured out my tale. I expected him to react in rage and sorrow, fully expected that he would send messengers to Hades ordering him to release my daughter. But his face was as hard as that rock there. Not a glimmer of sympathy did he show. When I had finished my tale, he said simply that he would take the matter under advisement, and that he would let me know his decision later. Later! Later!" She pounded her chest. "That delicate flower of a child will wither away in dark Tartarus. She needs air, sunlight, birdsong. Not darkness and smoke and the screams of the tormented. I couldn't believe how Zeus was acting, couldn't accept what he was saying. Then I saw that he had a new scepter: a magnificent volt-blue zigzag thunderbolt. And I understood that he had been bribed. That Hades had his pit demons dig up the rarest of metals and fashion this thunderbolt as a gift to the judge. Yes, the king of heaven and earth has been bribed; he will do no justice. My daughter must languish down there unless I can summon strength to save her."

"And how can I help you?" said Charon. "Your tale touches me, and I am prepared to make your enemies mine. But, although reasonably well grown, I am only a mortal, after all. What use can I be in a battle between gods?"

"You underestimate yourself," said Demeter. "I have heard tales of you, and now that I see you I understand that the tales have not been exaggerated. You are mortal, true, but of heroic size and gigantic strength—which means that you have a spark of divinity in you. I don't know your pedigree, but somewhere among your ancestors, I am sure, is a god or goddess who came down to earth long enough to love a mortal. Be that as it may, I have a specific use for you. I happen to know that you are the best and boldest ferryman in all the land. And I have learned that Hades is in dire need of a ferryman to transport the shades across the Styx. It is a treacherous, difficult job. All his ferrymen have been overcome by the sights they have seen and the sounds they have heard and have drowned themselves in the black river. You must go down there and apply for the post. There is no question but that you will be accepted. And then, having won Hades' trust, you will be able to serve me."

"And am I to be condemned to dwell forever in Tartarus, forever to cross and recross the Styx with boatload after boatload of miserable wailing shades? Is that not damnation before I am dead?"

"Damnation?" said Demeter, almost crooning, and laying her heavy hand upon his shoulder. Immediately he felt a strange new energy surging through him, a green, sappy strength seeming to flow from the very center of the earth, up through the soles of his feet and coursing through his huge body—a wild need to do what he had never done before, a marvelous carelessness of consequence. "Damned? Do you say damned?" crooned Demeter. "Why, in serving me so nobly you will earn my eternal gratitude. And the gratitude of all these poor wretches whom you will have saved from famine by returning the Spring Maiden to the earth. I shall pour blessings upon you. You shall live where you wish, do as you wish, enjoy enormous wealth and prestige and the endless thanks of all who will know what you have done."

"How about what I want now?" he said. "How about her?" He grasped Menthe by the arm.

"She shall be your companion, of course," said Demeter. "She shall go with you to Tartarus, down to the banks of the Styx itself, and there you shall find her waiting for you each time you cross and recross that fatal stream. Will you do it? Will you serve me? Will you unlock the crops by saving my daughter?"

"I'm yours," he said to Demeter. "Through hell and high water."

He strode off with Menthe at his side, her long legs matching him stride for stride.

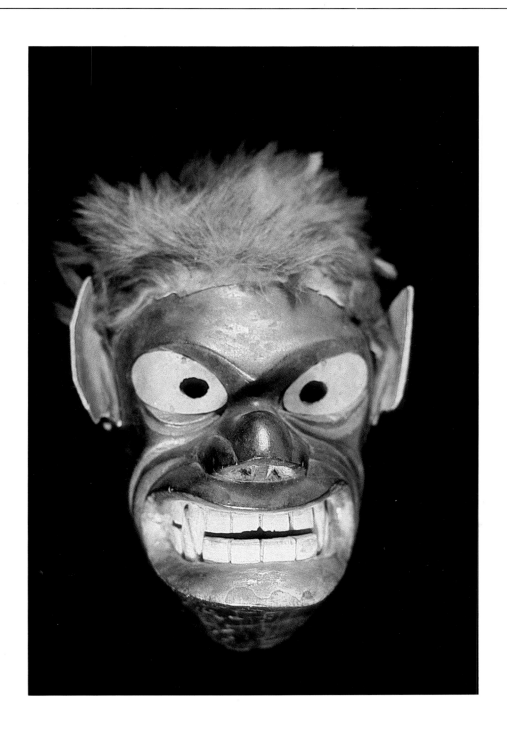

6

Infernal Plans

ades' underground realm was laced with veins of raw gold and silver, and held great troves of diamonds, rubies, sapphires. Here also had come a working party of those gigantic one-eyed smiths called Cyclopes. Master artisans, cousins to the gods, they chose to dwell in Hell because they could use its hotter flames for forge fires, and draw upon its hoard of gems and precious metals. There in their smithy they wrought the marvelous jewelry that Hades used to bribe Zeus when he had broken the divine code and wished to evade the penalties.

But after a thousand years of buying his way over, under, and through the law, Hades had come to know the High Judge very well. And knew that while Zeus could be bribed, he didn't always stay bribed. Hades also understood his sister, Demeter—knew how hot tempered and stubborn she was, how fiercely she doted on her daughter. So he was very much aware that the Harvest queen would shake heaven and trouble earth as she sought to reclaim Persephone and punish her abductor.

In short, Hades knew that because he had kidnapped the Spring Maiden he would be attacked from every quarter. And he prepared to defend himself.

He summoned a trusted adviser, a suave devil named Thanatos, and received him, not in his vast throne room, but on a basalt ledge overlooking the Lake of Fire. Here swam those shades who had been condemned to special punishment. Desperately, they breasted the flames trying to reach a shore that shrank away as they came near.

"Greetings, my lord," said Thanatos. "This is one of my favorite spots. It's so amusing to watch them swimming, burning, swimming, burning. The shore always recedes before them, but they never learn, do they?"

"Well, they're in agony," said Hades. "It doesn't much matter what they do. This was Hecate's favorite spot also, you know. She liked it because it's so high. From here she could watch over the widest part of my realm, and with her matchless eyesight could spot anyone breaking any rule even in the remotest corner of Hell. From here she would launch herself on golden wings, fall upon the offender, seize him in her claws, swing her stingray whip, and flay him down to the pulsing pink core."

"You miss her, don't you, my lord?"

"Aye, that I do," growled Hades. "But to think that she would trade the power and privilege of her office for life in a cave somewhere with her dribbling little scribbler. . . . I can't understand it."

"Neither can I," said Thanatos, who agreed with Hades on every possible occasion. "Can't understand it at all."

"What gripes me particularly," said Hades, "is that there was no one like her for keeping order down here. All my fiends and demons, trained for brutality though they are, were frightened by her very shadow, and didn't dare step out of line. Since she has been gone, though, they've been fighting among themselves, stealing from each other. Their pitchforks grow rusty, the roasting pits are cold, they neglect the shades who wander about, untormented. In general, things are going to heaven!"

Thanatos shuddered. Hades seldom cursed; when he did,

Hades knew that because he had kidnapped the Spring Maiden
he would be attacked from every quarter.

it meant that he was in a foul mood indeed, and that meant that anyone in the neighborhood would very soon be made to suffer. Thanatos was relieved when Hades did not smash his head in with his ebony scepter, but said:

"Another reason I need her now is that we shall soon be under attack. My shrieking shrew of a sister is raging up and down the earth and climbing Olympus to batter at the portals of the cloud castle, demanding that my realm be invaded and that my bride be taken from me by force. I shall resist, of course—unleash all the legions of Hell to keep what is mine. But in such warfare, Hecate would be invaluable to me."

"Invaluable," murmured Thanatos. "Uniquely so."

"We must replace her, don't you agree?"

"Oh, I agree, I agree! No one could agree more heartily. Replace her with whom?"

"That's where you come in, Thanatos."

"Me? As you know, my lord, I am ready to serve you with every last atom of my strength—and beyond. But I must admit, I'm not much of a fighter. Behind-the-lines strategy is more my style."

Hades almost smiled. "No, my chicken-livered hellion, I don't expect you to take her place. Of course not. What I want you to do is visit the Upper World and use all your cunning to find a replacement for Hecate. There must be some clever, ambitious monster somewhere whom I can train to rule the Harpies."

"Dark Majesty, I'm on my way!" cried Thanatos, hardly able to conceal his joy at being permitted to leave with his skull intact.

"Not so fast," growled Hades. "You're not going up there on a vacation, you know. Your orders are to put yourself in the way of the ablest monsters of earth and sea. Only by canvassing the entire roster of fearsome predators will you be able to find the one we want."

"O Hades," cried Thanatos, trying not to let his voice quaver, "in your service I shall make danger my business—and accomplish the task you have set me, or be devoured in the attempt."

He bowed low, and hurried off. Hades looked after him. "A coward," he thought. "But he fears me more than any monster imaginable, and such fear can be a spur. And his wits are as sharp as his heart is faint."

7

Advice Underseas

hanatos knew that the sea was a prime site for monsters, that most of them had been spawned there, even those who had climbed ashore. He also knew that Poseidon would welcome the feud between Hades and Demeter. The sea god liked the other gods to be at odds; it gave him a chance to raid their territories while they were fighting each other.

So Thanatos visited Poseidon in his great coral castle in the deepest part of the Ocean Stream. He gasped as he entered the enormous throne room, for it was as opulent as that of Hades, and much less gloomy. The silver and gold from the holds of sunken ships had been used to inlay floor and ceiling. The throne was of walrus-tusk ivory. Into the walls were cut great panes of crystal through which filtered the green light of undersea. Sharks and octopi glided past. Swordfish, balloon fish, and a shoal of lithe nereids pressed against the panes, smiling in.

And Poseidon was smiling as he sat on his throne. His crown was of gold and pearl, and pearls were braided into his green beard. His scepter was a trident.

"Welcome, Thanatos," he rumbled. "Do you come on embassy from my brother?"

"Welcome, Thanatos,"
he rumbled.

"Not exactly," said Thanatos, "but I do come on his business. It's a difficult matter, and I come to you, Moist Majesty, for counsel."

"Speak."

"As you may have heard, Hecate, Queen of the Harpies, has quit her post, and my master seeks a replacement. Now, your realm, so rich in so many ways, also abounds in monsters of all sizes, dispositions, and capacities."

"Hordes of 'em," said Poseidon. "We'll have to narrow the field. If this creature is to rule the Harpies and patrol Hell as Hecate did, it'll need wings, won't it? That rules out Ceto and Echidna and Ladon and the rest of the sea serpents. There are a pair of flying hags called Gorgons who are unpleasant enough to qualify as Harpies, but they've been exiled by their mother to the far northern wastes to guard their enchanted sister, Medusa. But that's another story. Anyway, they're not available. Besides, they're so ugly I don't think Hades could abide them for a second, no matter what service they could render. What else flies? Yes . . . there's another thing with wings—a very terrible thing I know only by reputation. Oh, I caught a glimpse of it once, but was too far away to be able to tell anything except that it was very big and moved with terrific speed. . . . Why do I call it *it*? It's a she."

"Does she dwell in the sea?"

"Not in my sea, nor in any of the cliffs girdling it. But did her hunting here, and I bear her a grudge. There used to be a pod of charming whales who would gather in a great chorus and sing at sunrise and dusk. Marvelous voices! In the evening they would come right here beyond those windows and serenade me. But that creature I'm telling you about—who's called the Sphinx, incidentally—formed a taste for them. Hunted them ruthlessly, I'm told, diving out of the sky and raking them up in her claws like a gull after herring. So they quitted this part of the sea and migrated to northern waters. Some instinct told them that the Sphinx hated the cold, and that they could hide from her in the icy depths. So they're gone, and she's gone too."

"Any idea where?"

"Rumor says that she burrows into the hot desert sand, in Egypt most likely. I don't know how much truth there is in the rumor. Nereids gossip ceaselessly, and make up what they don't know. But I give it to you for what it's worth."

"I thank you, Moist Majesty."

8

Dream-Tinkering

Thanatos hovered invisibly, watching a tribe called the Amaleki working itself into a frenzy. These were huge, ferocious warriors of the North African hill country who came into the desert once a year to catch mounts out of the wild camel herds. Not ordinary camels, but white racing stock, purebred. Astride these swift beasts, the Amaleki were the finest cavalry in that part of the world.

Now, in the valley that was their encampment, they were leaping and dancing about a bonfire, stoking themselves into the battle frenzy that had carried them to victory after victory. But their intention did not suit the plan that Thanatos had been spinning. He changed himself into a stone figure, and in a voice that was like a rock slide rumbled, "No!"

The tribesmen stopped dancing and stared in amazement. At first they saw nothing. The long, wavering shadows cast by the fire confused their sight. Thanatos came forward into the firelight. Immediately, the savage, bearded warriors fell to the ground, prostrating themselves.

One raised his head and spoke. He was their leader, Momo. "Welcome," he cried. "A thousand welcomes, O Nameless One.

He changed himself into a stone figure,
and in a voice that was like
a rock slide rumbled, "No!"

Thank you for appearing to your children, O God of Rock, carved from the central bone of Mother Earth. Thank you, thank you! Fill our bellies with courage and our arms with strength, for we go into battle against a monster that is devouring our camels. Bless us, bless us!"

"I come with more than blessings," boomed Thanatos. "I come with a gift of life. Yes, I give you back those lives you were about to throw away. You are to retire into the hills with the camels that remain to you, and leave the monster undisturbed. For if you go against her, who is called the Sphinx, you will surely die. Go, I say. Mount your camels and ride back into the hills—and think of new ways to praise me who has saved you from your own folly."

He vanished as suddenly as he had appeared. Hovered invisibly again, watching the tribesmen prod their camels awake, and gallop away.

Thanatos watched them until they had gone, then floated over the brown sands in search of the monster's burrow.

"I have deprived my master of many fine corpses this day," he said to himself. "But he will forgive me when he understands why I forbade the tribesmen to attack the Sphinx. He will understand that I had no wish to save their lives—far from it—but had to make sure that they did not disrupt her evening meal of camel and arouse her to fighting fury. I need her belly-full and deep asleep for my plan to work."

A dry riverbed called a *wadi* served as a burrow for the Sphinx. Bones littered its banks—the long leg bones and sharp rib cages and oval skulls of the camels she had devoured. Jackals searched the bones, cracking them for their last crumbs of marrow. The place stank. And Thanatos was grateful for the small wind that had arisen when the sun fell.

He moved upwind of the wadi and peered over its silted bank, and gasped at what he saw. "So the tales are true," he murmured. A lion's body she had, but of a lion as big as an elephant. Her head was hidden under her wing, and he couldn't see her face. Then she grunted and shifted, and in the bright moonlight he saw her face—that of a young woman—but her teeth were the fangs of a great cat. Her hair flowed cleanly back from her face and became a lion's mane.

He looked up. The stars flared like torches in the vast desert sky, and the moon seemed to be climbing as he watched. He raised his arms and began to spin, muttering as he spun.

Now, it must be understood that Thanatos was half brother to Hypnos, God of Sleep, and shared the family talent for dream management. It was this talent he now began to use in the service of his master.

He turned toward the north, singing wordlessly. In his song were the mingled voices of cold beasts—polar bear growl, seal bark, howl of the white wolf, cry of the great Arctic owl. The wind strengthened and swerved, and blew now from the north. An icy puff of it traveled down his outstretched arm and along his pointing finger—and blew down into the wadi, into the Sphinx's sleep.

She saw herself on the desert, in bright sunlight, moving toward her burrow. But the desert had changed. A wind scythed down from the north, lifting the sand into spouts. One of them whirled about her. And she, daughter of the sandstorm princess, whirled exultantly within it. But the old frenzied heat did not seize her; she was cold, horribly cold. The whirling cone was not sand; it was snow, fine granulated snow where no snow had ever fallen. She beat her wings, scattering the spout, and rushed toward her burrow.

But the riverbed had become a river again, and was frozen. Sunlight, hitting the strange ice, splintered and mingled with the blowing snow. Icy needles of light seemed to be aiming themselves at her very marrow. She shuddered deeply, half-knowing that she was asleep, hoping she was. She tried to awake, but could not. She was locked in sleep, caged in her dream, imprisoned in weird frost.

When Thanatos heard her utter a shuddering moan and heard the loud chattering of her fangs, he turned to face the south. The wind shifted, and was striped with hot airs. Thanatos directed the wind down into the wadi where it blew into the Sphinx's sleep and thawed her dream.

The snow was gone. She was in a different place, hotter than the desert, and more interesting. Almost too hot. But not quite. She stretched blissfully. She seemed to be perched on a basalt ledge overlooking a lake of fire. Steam arose, a great cloud of it. She couldn't quite see the swimmers, but knew they were there, for she heard their screams. And these shrieks of agony seemed to belong to the heat. It was *diabolical* heat, suiting her completely.

She spread her wings and flew off the ledge to explore the

place. She saw twisted, frothing demons wielding pitchforks, herding pale shades toward the open roasting pits. She floated low over the pits, feeling the heat of their fire. It was good, very good; she was where she wanted to be. But she wasn't quite sure where that was.

Then, still half-knowing that she was asleep, but hoping now that she wasn't, she saw someone prowling the margin of her dream. And the fiery landscape slowly began to close like the

She couldn't quite see the swimmers, but knew they were there, for she heard their screams. And these shrieks of agony seemed to belong to the heat.

HELL Canto 22.

iris of an eye, focusing on the black-caped figure. And she knew that she must shake herself awake and give herself to the instructions of this one who traveled freely over the frontiers of sleep, and who alone could tell her what her dream meant.

She found herself awake in her burrow under the pulsing stars. She lurched out of the wadi and stood among the grinning camel skulls. She looked up and saw the cloaked figure floating above her, black as a cutout against the moon.

"Who are you?" she croaked.

"I am Thanatos, who serves Hades, Lord of the Land Beyond Death."

"Hell?"

"Some call it Hell."

"Is that where my dream took me—that blissful, flaming realm?"

"It was."

"Did you send the dream?"

"I did."

"Why?"

"Because my master may ask you to make your home there, and serve in a very important post."

"What post?"

"Queen of the Harpies, who were formerly led by Hecate."

"Yes, yes! Let's go down there!"

"Not so fast. My master likes what he has heard about you, but his standards are very high. He will want to examine you first, and perhaps set you a task so that you may prove yourself."

"I'm ready to meet him."

"No, you are not."

"What do you mean?"

"Hecate was hellishly intelligent, you know. If you expect to replace her you will have to become as powerful in mind as you are in body. Before meeting Hades you must hone your wits and accumulate knowledge."

"Oh, I don't know. That's not my line at all."

"Make it your line."

"But how?"

"That *how* is the first of your tasks."

"Impossible! I can't do it."

"Before giving up, be aware that we have informed ourselves of your tastes and have stocked the Styx with singing whales."

"Singing whales? Really?"

"Frisky beasts. Keep capsizing the ferry. We've lost some veteran boatmen and shoals of shades."

"You're making me hungry."

"And the silvery apes. Oh, my dear monster, you have no idea of the amount of effort we spent rounding them up. They're almost extinct, you know. We had to literally snatch the last of them out of a jungleful of ravening tigers and leopards. If you do join us, we'll set up a breeding farm to raise a fine population of silvery apes."

"Singing whales . . . silvery apes. I must put myself among those toothsome creatures; I must, I must! I'm off, Thanatos— on my way to hone my wits and gain knowledge. Not that I know how."

"Perhaps greed will teach you. Good hunting."

9

An Unwilling Bride

ades was having a hard time with his flower maiden. Accustomed to being obeyed in all things, he was confused by her resistance. He went to great lengths to please her. In his kingdom lay the world's trove of gold and silver, of diamonds and rubies and sapphires. He heaped her with jewelry and had his slaves spin her gowns of silver and gold thread. He called out the nimblest of acrobats, the most graceful dancers, and the sweetest singers from among his shades to provide her with entertainment. Still she would not speak to him, would not look at him—nor would she eat.

And her resistance fueled his desire until it was a raging furnace. He didn't know what to do. He didn't dare use force; he knew it wouldn't work. Cold as an icicle now, this radiant slip of a goddess, he knew that if he tightened his grasp she would, like an icicle, change form and vanish. For all his vicious temper, though, the Lord of the Underworld had great control over himself. Boiling within, he let nothing show.

Still determined to please her, he sent instructions to the smithy. The Cyclopes hammered out a great sheet of gold leaf, shaped it into an enormous globe, and punched it full of holes. The globe was cunningly hinged so that it opened like a shell,

She turned and strolled toward the cypress grove.

allowing smiths to insert torches. And these fatwood torches were lighted by fire taken from the very center of the earth—the primal flame, hot as the sun.

Light streamed out of the golden shell, fiery light. And this he had done, Hades told Persephone, so that she might be warmed by artificial sun and feel more at home underground. But Persephone did not thank him, nor smile, nor say anything, but did look him in the face and hold his gaze for a moment. Then she turned and strolled toward the cypress grove. But, he noticed, she did stop before the tree line and lift her face into the new golden light.

And this was a bit of comfort to him, but not enough.

As Persephone basked in the jeweled light of the artificial sun, she saw someone approaching. The figure was so tall she thought it must be Hades coming after her. She tensed, preparing to dart into the grove and lose herself among the trees. But then she saw that it was not Hades, but a mortal. A massive youth in a torn tunic. He was followed by one of the nymphs who had attended her in the meadows of home. The youth approached. He had a thatch of red hair. His arms and legs were cables of strength; his neck one column of muscle. And to the scorched air he brought an aroma of the Upper World—of a river and real sunshine and free wind. His voice was slow and deep; he spoke as one who used words rarely.

"Are you the goddess Persephone?"

"I am. Who are you?"

"My name is Charon. I bear a message from your mother. Eat nothing."

She widened her eyes. "Really?"

"Or perhaps you have already?"

"No, sir." She smiled at him. "And I'm getting very hungry."

"I'm sure you must be, missy. But I'm only telling you what your mother told me to say."

"And very good of you, young sir, to bring me a message. Have you had a long journey?"

"From Eleusis."

"Yes, a very long one. But you're so big and strong you can probably do even harder things."

He didn't say anything. He was too busy staring. She was clad in the colors of spring flowers; her hair was yellow as forsythia, her eyes like wet violets, and she wore a tunic of lilac and rose. And when she had drawn cat faces on pansies it was after gazing at her own image in a pool.

"Why are you looking at me like that?"

*He had a thatch
of red hair.*

"Like what?"

"Staring. . . ."

"You're so pretty, I guess."

Persephone looked at the nymph who was standing behind Charon. She recognized her now; her name was Menthe. She had been one of those who had attended the April Maiden as she plied her paintbrush among the wildflowers, and Persephone had always been fond of the big, vital wench, but now, suddenly, she disliked her.

"Menthe," she said. "Why don't you go off a bit—toward the castle, say—and warn us if anyone approaches. I wish to have a private conversation with my mother's messenger."

The nymph smiled a small smile, then curtsied so low it seemed almost like mockery—but arose and glided over the black grass toward the castle. Persephone looked after her, and said:

"D'you think she's pretty, too?"

"Menthe?"

"Who else could I mean? Do you?"

"Yes."

"Prettier than me?"

"No."

"As?"

He shook his head slowly. "Nobody is, I guess."

"That's all right then," said Persephone. "Now tell me exactly what my mother said."

"Oh, she said a lot of things. I can't remember all of it. She was very angry—screaming and hollering and throwing famines around. But what she told me to tell you was 'Don't eat—and your mother will save you.' "

"How long am I supposed to go on starving?"

"She didn't say. But you won't starve to death because you're a goddess and can't die."

"How about you, large youth? I suppose now that you've delivered your message you'll scoot back up with your hussy. . . . Well, when you and she are stuffing yourselves with roast lamb and lentils and cheese and olives and honey, just think of me down here, growing thinner and sadder, thinner and sadder. Even if goddesses can't die, they can suffer, you know."

"We're not going anywhere, Princess. I'm to stay here and man a ferry across that ugly black river, and be ready to help you when the time comes. And Menthe will attend you, if you like."

10

Instructing the Sphinx

The Sphinx finally sent word by Hermes, the messenger god, that she had prepared herself to meet Hades and would soon be there. Thanatos hastened to the throne room.

"She's on her way, my lord," he said, "but you won't enjoy her company."

"Eh?"

"To put it plainly, the Sphinx stinks."

"We're used to strange smells here—charred souls, basted sins, ashy tears. When did you get so finicky?"

"We've never experienced anything like her stench, O King. The lion-smell of sulphur, dung, and rotting meat, but multiplied a thousand times."

"Oh well, I'll make her keep her distance. Have someone carry my instructions to her. You, perhaps, Thanatos. I hereby appoint you special envoy to the creature. Don't shudder; I'm only joking. We'll get one of the Harpies to do it."

"Thank you, Majesty."

"Besides, I must tell you that my bride-to-be, the Flower Princess, will envelop me in such fragrance that no unpleasant odor will penetrate."

"A very pretty sentiment, my lord. Shall I simply then take the Sphinx to you when she gets here?"

"Well," said Hades, "why don't you bring her by way of the Styx? Tell her it's my wish that she swim across rather than fly over. That strong river should wash away some of the stench."

Just past the black iron gates that are the portals of Hell stood a grove of trees—cypress and alder, and within that grove gushed a crystal fountain. Lethe's spring it was, where the newly dead would stop to drink, and immediately forget everything that happened while they were alive. Before the Sphinx arrived, Thanatos filled a bucket at this fountain and poured it into the Styx.

"A hideous smell," he said to himself, "may after all be only the memory of corruption. Perhaps a bucketful of forgetfulness will wash the spoor of foul meals from the Sphinx's body."

It may be that his idea worked. For it is reported that Hades received the Sphinx without flinching, and listened courteously as she told him that she wished to take Hecate's place as Queen of the Harpies.

"There is much to consider," said Hades. "Hecate, you must realize, was not only a matchless fighter but also extremely intelligent. In fact, she was my chief aide, and often counseled me on matters of policy. Now, I must say, you look like you can handle yourself in a fight, but do you have it up here?" He tapped his head. "No offense, but Hecate was positively brilliant, and anyone who seeks to take her place—well, you understand."

The Sphinx said: "I understood that before I came down, Your Majesty. And have tried to prepare myself for the job. Have been trying to add to my own stock of intelligence in a very direct way—by eating the cleverest people I could find."

"Indeed? A novel approach. Tell me more."

"Well, I had mixed results at first. Poets didn't agree with me—too sweet. Political theorists gave me gas. But I kept trying, and found that mathematicians were the dish. They stick to the ribs. I ate a whole school of them and suffered no indigestion whatsoever. The only thing was I found myself getting passionate about puzzles—became positively addicted to riddles. But to sum it up, I do believe I'm brainy enough now to fill the post."

"You found poets too sweet, eh?"

"Quite nauseating."

"Well, I have a bitter one for you—who also happens to be of a different order of intelligence from all the others you have engorged. Hearken now, you'll need more than logic; you'll need imagination to lead the Harpies and impose my discipline upon the legions of Hell. You'll need to balance your diet with this poet."

"Who is he? Where do I find him?"

"His name is Thallo. You'll find him somewhere on Crete."

Hades didn't tell her that Thallo was wedded to Hecate. What he wanted, of course, was for Thallo to be killed so that Hecate, unattached, would return to Tartarus.

"They'll fight, no doubt," he said to himself, "this Sphinx creature and Hecate. And a splendid sight their battle should be. If Hecate wins, all the better. If this one wins, then I'll allow her to take Hecate's place. For no loser can queen it over the Harpies."

11

Another Abduction

he Sphinx flew toward Crete, where Hecate dwelt now with her little husband. Their home was a cave halfway up the slope of Mount Ida, not far from that great cavern called earth's womb—so named because here was where Rhea had given birth to Zeus, shaking the mountain and starting an avalanche in her mighty labor.

As it happened, while the Sphinx was flying to Crete, Hecate was winging away from it, heading for Libya on some mysterious errand of her own. Now, it is not quite clear how word got out that the Sphinx had left Tartarus and was on her way to the Upper World to catch Thallo and eat him raw. It may have been Hades himself who passed the word so that Hecate might hear of it and prepare to fight. In any case, the news traveled faster than the Sphinx could fly, and reached Thallo by way of some gossipy dryads. He was in the forest dancing with them at the time—something he could do only when Hecate was elsewhere. It was hard for him to stop dancing; the dryads were beautiful and very playful. But with the monster en route, he knew he had to make plans very fast.

He thought and thought, but could think of no possible

way he could escape the Sphinx if she caught sight of him. "So I must hide from her, but how? Not in my cave; she'll force someone to tell her where it is, then dig me out. And outside the cave I'm a goner too. An eagle, it is said, can spot a rabbit from a mile up, and this creature is supposed to be an even better hunter. So, no place to hide. I'll have to find another way. What way? Where's that wonderful imagination of mine when I really need it? Is it good only for word slinging and such trifles? Let's see now . . . what do I know about her? She wants to eat me, I know that—a dreadful piece of knowledge. Is there some way I can make her not want to? Is there anything that she'd refuse to eat? Aha, there may be. Beef! She is cousin to the beast gods of Egypt, and the most potent of them is Hathor of the Horned Moon, the great cow goddess, whose milk is rain. And Hathor's flesh is sacred, and cows and bulls partake of this holiness, and are not to be harmed.

"Can I be sure of this? Well, the eldest tales say so. And as a poet I have to believe them. Let's hope this monster shares my belief. If not, I'm in deep trouble, and Hecate will have to find another husband when she comes home from Libya. There are many bigger, stronger, handsomer men than I—and almost anyone is braver. But I seem to be the only one who can make her laugh. So I'll have to try to keep alive for her sake, not to mention my own. Bulls ho!"

And he scampered down the mountain and headed for Knossos, where a herd of magnificent bulls was kept for the sport called bull dancing. This was a weekly entertainment demanded by the king. It was welcomed by the populace also—for the king's other sport was torturing his subjects.

"I'll hide myself among the herd," said Thallo to himself. "If my theory's correct, the Sphinx will refuse to hunt me there for fear of harming one of the creatures sacred to Hathor. Of course, there's another danger attached to this plan. Hecate has warned me in the harshest possible terms to keep my distance from the lithe and lovely girls who somersault through the bulls' horns in the fourth turn of the dance. If she catches me anywhere near the ring, she promises, she'll turn me over her knee and blister my bottom in full view of the dancers. But what's a spanking by my dear wife, even a shameful public one, compared to being eaten raw by the Sphinx?"

Thus ran his thoughts as he trotted along the shore of the shining sea toward Knossos. But this set him thinking of something else: How Hecate, in moments of violent affection, would swoop upon him, clutch him in her claws, and lift him into the air, kissing and caressing him in midflight. Then he thought: "But the Sphinx, they say, falls like a thunderbolt from a clear sky as she swoops upon her prey. Suppose she falls upon me suddenly and snatches me up as an eagle does a lamb. I'll feel myself lifted into the air, feel her mouth upon me, and think for a moment,

She stood over him,
considering.

57

perhaps, that it is Hecate—but then realize that the mouth is not kissing my neck but throttling it. One last glimpse of the sun as I struggle in her claws, then the mountain spinning beneath me—then the breath will be crushed out of me. Everything will go black, fade into nothingness. . . ."

And, in his poet's way, the thought in his head became realer than reality, and he frightened himself into a deep swoon. And was lying there unconscious when the Sphinx spotted him, and dived.

She stood over him, considering. "Shall I eat him here? I've just had a flock of sheep and am not very hungry. And if I should eat him now, how do I know that this weird wit of his that Hades described will really enter my own thinking? Poets have always given me indigestion. This one's supposed to be bitter rather than sweet, but who knows? Poetry is poetry, and I loathe it. And I must say, this bard looks particularly scrawny and unappetizing. Besides, if I should eat him and his so-called imagination doesn't take, then when I go back to Tartarus, Hades will simply think I'm lying, that I didn't catch him at all, and will be furious with me. I know: I'll take him back to Tartarus, to the castle in Erebus, into the throne room itself, and there devour him as Hades watches. That way there will be no misunderstanding."

With quickening interest,
Thallo realized that he recognized these mountains.

She seized the unconscious Thallo and bore him off like a gull taking a fish.

When Thallo came out of his swoon he found himself clutched in an enormous clawed paw, and saw jagged peaks sliding beneath him. Looking up, he saw huge wings blotting the sun. Slung between them was the underbelly of a gigantic lioness. But she wore a woman's face, quite young; her mouth gleamed with a lion's fangs.

Too much. Utter terror. He tried to swoon again. He could not; his heart was beating too hard. The wind was cooled by snow as it whistled past the peaks—was then warmed by the noonday sun and spurted into updrafts. The Sphinx rode those updrafts like a sea bird bobbing on the surf.

With quickening interest, Thallo realized that he recognized these mountains. They belonged to the Saronic range near Mycenae, and he had wandered them as a youth, climbing them to see the wonder of snow and to dance with oreades. One slope, however, no youth dared climb; even the goatherds shunned it. For in one of its clefts had nestled a lake called Avernus. This, according to ancient legend, Hades had chosen as his entrance to the Underworld. Had emptied the lake of its blue waters, and broken through its bed, making a chasm that led down, down, through a chain of interlocking caves, to the shore of the Styx.

And now, Thallo realized, the Sphinx had begun to coast in a slant dive toward that very chasm. "Avernus?" he thought. "Is she really going there? Is it possible she's taking me to Tartarus, where only the dead may enter? She knows I'm still alive, of course. And, of course, intends to render me defunct before reaching the Styx. She won't have to bother; I'm about to die of fear."

Nevertheless, he knew he wouldn't. For some reason he felt throbbingly alive. "How wonderful," he thought, "if I could actually get into the place with all my me-ness intact."

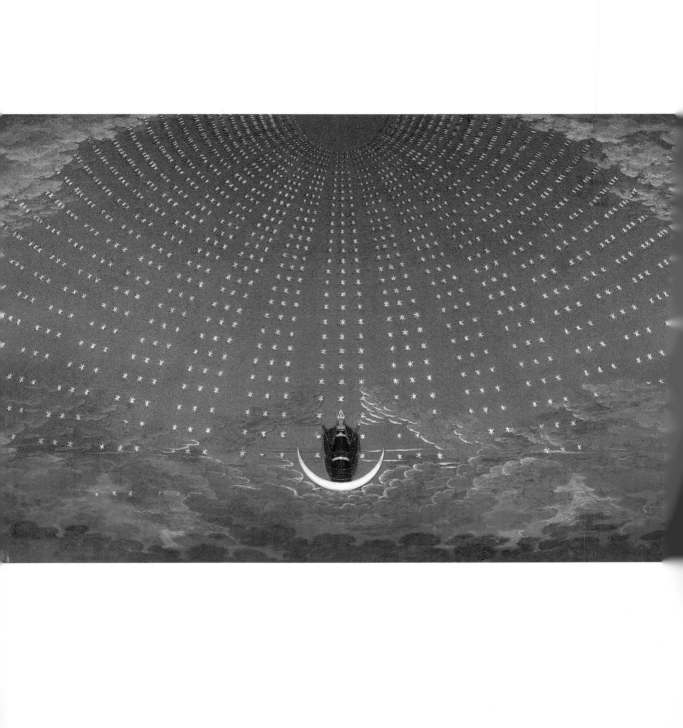

12

Demeter Strikes

he Garden of the Gods lay on the sunny southern slope of Olympus, and was the pleasantest spot in the entire world. Botanus, the hundred-handed giant who was head gardener, had ransacked the earth for the most gorgeous, most fragrant blooms and had transplanted them here. For this place, too, Demeter in happier days had decreed an eternal June, so that no plant withered, no bush died, and the birds sang always.

Upon this day, however, Hera, entering the garden, was horrified at what she saw. She turned and charged up the slope and into the cloud castle, searching for her husband.

"Zeus!" she screamed. "Make her stop!"

"Make *who* stop *what*?"

"Our sister! Demeter! She's in the garden, uprooting all our plants, and swears she won't let them grow again until her daughter is returned."

"That damned old shrew!" growled Zeus. "She's caused me a lot of trouble lately. Been withholding her crops down there . . . and the complaints of the hungry are beginning to deafen the statues in all my temples."

"Well, why don't you make Hades send back her stupid daughter?"

"A matter of policy, my dear, high policy," mumbled Zeus, who had accepted a bribe from Hades, and was beginning to regret it. "Go down to the garden and tell her to leave immediately or feel the full weight of my wrath."

"Won't work, my lord. She's even angrier than you are, and is demanding justice."

"I dislike injustice," said Zeus. "And dislike its victims even more. Make tremendous pests of themselves; ever notice . . . . Very well, tell her to come here and I'll discuss things with her. And tell her she'd better bloody well replant everything she's pulled up or I'll throw her off the mountain."

The conversation was held, and Demeter was all smiles as she left the cloud castle. She hurried to Hermes and cried, "Go to Zeus! He has an errand for you, a most urgent one! You are to go to Tartarus and in the master's name demand the release of my daughter. Will you ride with me to the Gates of Hell? I have the swiftest horse in the world, given me by Poseidon."

"Thank you, Aunt," said Hermes. "But I believe that my winged sandals are even faster."

We have seen how Hades hung an artificial sun to please his bride. But he was even prouder of the night he had contrived. The roots of mountains are the rafters of Hell, and to these black beams he had fastened diamonds to imitate stars. Among them, he hung a moon of purest silver. He stood with Persephone in the courtyard of his jet and ruby palace, inviting her to admire his jeweled sky.

"Those are diamonds," he said, pointing up.

She didn't answer.

"They could be emeralds or sapphires if you'd like a bit more color."

She shrugged.

"You like diamonds, eh? Well, choose the ones you want

and my Cyclopes will unpin them from the sky and make a necklace for you. Unless you'd prefer a bracelet. You needn't choose; you can have both.''

This time she didn't even shrug but turned from him and looked into the distance. She was expecting Charon this evening and was trying to hide her excitement. She knew that her secret would be fatal to the young boatman if Hades guessed.

Just then Hades heard a ringing herald shout, and knew that Hermes had come. He was not pleased. Hermes traveled to the Underworld each day, leading the unbodied spirits there. But he left them on the far shore of the Styx and never entered Tartarus itself if he could help it. When he did it was to bring some message from Zeus, usually an unwelcome one. Displeased though he was, Hades received his nephew graciously.

"Welcome, Hermes. To what do we owe the pleasure of so rare a visit?"

"Official business, I'm afraid," said Hermes. "I come at the order of Father Zeus."

"Ah," said Hades. "He wishes to congratulate me on my betrothal, no doubt. And you wish to add your good wishes to his."

"Not quite," said Hermes. "It is his command that you release Persephone into my custody so that I may conduct her to the Upper World and return her to her mother."

"Nonsense," said Hades. "There must be some mistake. The last time I saw Zeus, he agreed that I might keep her for my own."

"Things have changed," said Hermes. "Demeter has per-suaded him otherwise. The only way you can hold her here is if she has signified her consent by eating something. Has she?"

Hades knew that she hadn't, but said: "I don't know."

"Where is she, by the way?"

"Somewhere about. She was just here."

Indeed, Persephone was quite close, but out of sight. When

she heard Hermes shouting she had slid behind a myrtle tree, and stood there listening to every word. She didn't know why she had hidden herself; she had done it by reflex. Having so bossy a mother had taught her to be secretive. Now she felt a pang of joy as she saw Charon's red head blazing in the artificial moonlight. She sprang out, seized his hand, and drew him behind the myrtle.

"Charon, Charon," she whispered. "We're leaving!"

He stared at her in amazement.

"Yes, yes, it's true! That's why Hermes is here—to take me home. You'll be coming too, of course."

She moved away, startled, as rage twisted his face. His huge hands were closing and unclosing, as if seeking someone to throttle.

"What's wrong?" she cried.

"I can't leave."

"Why not?"

"I just vowed to serve Hades for a thousand years."

"Why? Why?"

"Only way I could get permission to stay. I thought you were staying. I didn't think he'd ever let you go. In fact, I don't see how he can bear to."

"That's very sweet to say." She took his hand again. "What does it matter what you promised? Just break it."

He shook his head. "It's a sacred vow—unbreakable. But if you go to the Upper World I'll manage to get away every few months and come see you."

"Not good enough. I want to see you every day."

"All right," he muttered. "I'll break the damned vow."

She studied his face for a moment, then lifted her slender hand and stroked it, smiling her first grown-up smile. "No, my darling," she said. "You're all one piece, a splendid one, but inflexible. If you break your vow you'll break your heart. And if yours breaks, so will mine."

"What shall we do then?"

"I'll do what you did, stay because you can't go."

"You here in this gloomy place, forever?"

"Together we'll light up our own space. Besides, I am what I am, wherever I am. And will bring a bit of April to this accursed place."

"But if you stay, he'll make you his bride."

"Ah, but you and I will know different, won't we? And it's what we know that counts. Anyway, this gives me an excuse to break my stupid fast. Let's go into the orchard and pick some fruit."

As they left, they heard Hades saying: "I need five days, old chap. Just five. I'm about to stage a monstrous battle between Hecate and the Sphinx. It will be a magnificent spectacle. I'm inviting all the gods to attend. I'm sure I'll be able to get Zeus to see things my way while he's down here. Just five days."

"I don't have the authority, Uncle," said Hermes. "My orders were clear."

Hades was still trying to persuade him when he saw Persephone strolling out of the orchard, and he was overjoyed to see her holding a split pomegranate. Her mouth was stained with its red juice. So pleased was he that he neglected to scowl at Charon, whose boatmanship he valued but whose too frequent presence was beginning to irk him.

Hermes took in the situation at a glance. "Congratulations, Uncle!" he cried, and flew off, ankle wings whirring.

13

Chaining a Poet

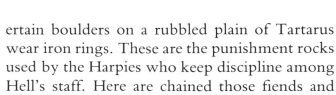

ertain boulders on a rubbled plain of Tartarus wear iron rings. These are the punishment rocks used by the Harpies who keep discipline among Hell's staff. Here are chained those fiends and demons who have broken some rule or other and need flogging. And it was to one of these rocks that the Sphinx shackled Thallo when she brought him to Tartarus.

She left him there and went off to present herself to Hades. Thallo did not act like a captive. He had expected to be finished off long before this, and was delighted to find himself uneaten. He lounged against his rock and stared across the dismal plain. Figures fledged themselves out of the mist, hardly thicker than fog. These were the shades; they were what was left of those who had died. Thallo studied them keenly, for whatever they had become, he knew, he would become too—probably very soon.

He was disappointed in them. He had expected shades, *souls*, to be purer, more concentrated, now that they had shed their flesh. But these vaporous things seemed very cold, indifferent to everything except themselves. They didn't even glance his way, but drifted past, twittering.

Hades did not wish to meet the Sphinx indoors, even in so vast a hall as his throne room. He received her then upon the

Plain of Pain, halfway between the Gutwinder and the Marrow Log.

"I caught Thallo," said the Sphinx. "And brought him here so that you might watch me eat him, and see how strictly I follow your suggestions."

"Where is he?"

"In that field yonder, chained to a rock."

"Let's keep him alive for a bit," said Hades. "Hecate will be coming to claim him, which will give you the chance you've been waiting for—to fight her in single combat for the queenship of the Harpies."

"Is that the chance I've been waiting for?"

"Why, certainly! I should hope so. How can you really prove yourself fit for the post except by challenging the one who held it?"

"I see," said the Sphinx. "I guess I didn't quite understand. Doesn't matter. I'm ready to fight her, or anyone else. No one—bird, beast, fish, hero or monster—has lasted more than a few minutes against me."

"Glad to hear it," said Hades. "She's undefeated too. Should be a good match. I've invited the entire Pantheon to view it. Incidentally, I said 'single combat,' and that's how it'll probably end, but you'll both have allies."

"Indeed? What for?"

"To serve me the way I require, my Harpy queen must show generalship, you know. I don't just want to see how well you fight, but how well you lead troops. So you'll have troops. And to make it fair, she'll have some too."

"Who'll be on my side?"

"I have a unique bestiary down here. And giants and dragons, and a staff of assorted fiends and demons. You can have first choice."

"Very well," said the Sphinx. "I choose the Harpies, the

hundred-handed giants, the dragons, and the First Torture Team."

"That leaves only Cerberus, the Manglers, the serpents, and the Cyclopes. And the Cyclopes are doubtful. They prefer to fight only in their own interests. They may simply lean on their mallets and watch."

"All the better," said the Sphinx. "Who wants to be fair in a fight?"

"You lack experience," said Hades, "but seem to have the right hellish instincts. Good enough, then. Go meet your troops. Hecate should be here by tomorrow."

Chained to his rock, peering through the mist, Thallo was too interested to be unhappy. He was alive, alive among the dead, something he had felt before when wandering the slopes of Hel-

He found himself watching a weird
carnival—the Hell tales
told him by Hecate
fledging themselves out
in the dreamy mist.

icon with his fellow bards, whose verse was so much feebler than his own.

Elated by strangeness, filling with a sense of unfamiliar power, he found himself watching a weird carnival—the Hell tales told him by Hecate fledging themselves out in the dreamy mist. He saw the swooping Harpies she had led; the bat-winged Furies who were even worse; the drifting, twittering shades driven by pitchfork demons and roasted by turnspit demons; the gigantic, gliding serpents she had admired because they had no cruelty, only blind strength. And here he was set down in this taboo place among such fabled creatures—himself, wildly curious, furiously observant, alive among the dead.

Now a flock of ghosts shuddered past, driven by a pair of demons. As they wielded their pitchforks, driving the shades along, the demons chatted about the great battle that was to be staged between Hecate and the Sphinx. Thallo tried desperately to hear what they were saying. He ran toward them until his chain jerked him back. Their slurred infernal accent was hard to understand. He strained his ears so hard that his eyes bulged. He finally understood most of what they said. He slumped back against the rock, thinking hard. Hecate was coming for him; that much was clear, but she would not be allowed to leave before fighting the Sphinx—and an array of fearsome allies.

He saw a huge figure shouldering through the mist, and felt a warm thrill of recognition. Even at this distance he knew that whoever was coming toward him was a living mortal.

"Greetings!" he shouted.

The figure approached, loomed before him, and Thallo knew who it was from the tales he had heard.

"What are you doing here?" said the youth. "You're no shade."

"Indeed I'm not. At least not quite yet. Neither are you. You're the wild young ferryman from the Alpheus, here on a mission from Demeter."

"How the hell do you know so much about me?"

"People tell me things. And I'm delighted to meet you, Charon. You and I are the only warm bodies in this dank place. Why don't you loose me from this rock like a good fellow?"

Charon took the chain between his hands and snapped it as if it were twine.

"Thank you," said Thallo. "You're wonderfully strong. Whom will you be helping in the great fight—Hecate or the Sphinx?"

"Neither. I'm strictly neutral. Won't even be on this side of the Styx. I'll moor my boat on the far shore and watch things from there. Farewell."

He turned and strode off.

"Wait!" called Thallo. "May I come visit you on the ferry?"

Charon didn't answer, but walked away into the mist.

14

Before the Battle

he great chasm of Avernus is not the only way into Death's realm. There is also a secret passage—a rocky shaft leading from the bottom of a burned-out volcano and entering Tartarus from the south. Hecate took this back way and came into Hell before she was expected.

A friendly fiend told her where to find her husband. She clove the murky air like an arrow, and spotted him sitting on a rock from which dangled a broken chain. He was scribbling on a bit of parchment. She swooped, scooped him up, hugging him until his ribs almost cracked, kissing his face. Alighting on the rock, she held him on her lap, enfolded in her wings. Rocked him back and forth, crooning:

"Oh pettikins . . . I was afraid she'd eaten you."

"Not yet. Soon, she thinks."

"I'll give her something to chew on that'll break her damned jaws," snarled Hecate. Then she sighed. "It won't be easy, though. She's very big. And has a host of wicked fighters on her side."

"Like to hear some of my ideas?"

"I love your ideas, poopsie, but what do you know about fighting?"

"I know things about the Sphinx. When I learned that she was hungering for my acquaintance I tried to learn everything I could. Picked up a few facts and even more rumors. Then, of course, she gave me more time than I wanted to observe her closely."

"Tell me what you know. But whisper, baby. Spies simply swarm down here. Hades actually has a flock of flying ears—look like fleshy bats. And detachable eyes that skitter about on their lashes like water bugs."

He pulled down her head and pushed aside her hair to whisper into her ear. She listened intently and smiled at him when he finished. But it was a grim smile.

"What do you think?" he whispered.

"I don't know, sweetling. You're quite a little strategist. But . . ."

"But what?"

"It's a desperate gamble. Disaster if it doesn't work."

"Well, I mean it only as a last resort."

"It'll be last all right—for her or me. But worth trying if everything else fails."

He tried to slide out of her arms.

"Where are you going?"

"To find Charon. He's the key to it."

"Stay a minute."

He knew what she meant but could not say—that these were probably their last minutes together. Choking back a sob, he rushed off. She spread her wings and rose into the air.

Using a giant's rusty helmet as a bucket, Charon was dipping water from the Styx and sloshing it over the lower deck. Thallo sat cross-legged on the upper deck, watching.

"Can't really clean this cruddy old barge," said Charon. "And it'll be carrying a lot of important passengers—the whole bloody Pantheon and a mob of minor gods—to see the fight, you know."

"Which takes us back to what we were talking about," said Thallo.

"No use going back," said Charon. "I've told you a dozen times I'm staying out of that fight. There's no reason for me to help your spooky wife against that other weirdo with wings."

"There is a reason. Hecate left Hell because she cared for someone. You entered Hell because you cared for someone. You and she have the only two loving hearts in this place of death. You should support each other."

"Sounds pretty," said Charon. "But it's not a good enough reason for me to get into that mess. I'm in enough trouble down here."

"Yes. And your trouble is another reason you should help Hecate. I warn you—if the Sphinx wins this fight and becomes Queen of the Harpies, she will be used by Lord Hades to keep strict watch on you and Persephone. You'll never be able to meet."

Charon poured a helmetful of water over his head to help him think more clearly. "Stop," he growled. "I don't want to hear any more."

A sound came to them; it was like a huge collective sigh. They saw Hermes herding the day's draft of shades. They weren't used to being dead yet; they moaned and chittered, shrank back from the black waters. Thallo watched, fascinated. He had no idea why Hermes was waving some of the shades forward with his snake-entwined staff, and held others back. The ones who came forward climbed aboard the ferry. The others were driven to the river by Hermes. They shuddered into the water and were carried by a sideways current toward the shore where loomed the Gates of Hell. Vultures dived because some of the swimmers still wore rags of flesh.

Thallo jumped ashore as Charon unmoored the ferry. He had to find out why some shades rode while others swam. He looked up at Hermes who, balancing on ankle wings, stood on air—so youthful and radiant that Thallo fell to his knees before him.

"O Bright God," he cried. "Tell me, please, why do you divide the shades upon this shore? What is your principle of selection?"

"A universal principle," said Hermes. "One affecting gods and mortals. They ride who can pay the fare; others swim. That is why those who can afford it cover corpses' eyes with gold pieces; those who can't curse their poverty but please the gods by praying more fervently than those who are able to send their relatives off in style."

"Thank you," said Thallo. "I understand perfectly."

"Now a word for you, Thallo. You are alive, and on the far shore of the Styx. You are free to leave, if you wish, and I shall conduct you back to the Upper World."

"I thank you again, but I must stay. My wife, Hecate, as you may know is about to engage in deadly combat with the Sphinx."

"That's a reason for you to leave, not to stay. If your wife loses, the Sphinx will simply drag you before Hades' throne and eat you raw. If Hecate wins, she will be invited to resume the queenship of the Harpies."

"Yes, I know," said Thallo. "I've considered all that, and have made my choice. I haven't always been a good husband, but she seems somehow to have sunk her talons into the very

He looked up at Hermes who,
balancing on ankle wings,
stood on air.

center of my being. And I would have no interest in keeping alive if she weren't with me. So, if she is destroyed by the Sphinx, or if she chooses to stay here and queen it over those flying hags again, then I'll simply shed my empty life as a snake moults its skin. I'll become a shade and abide with her forever."

"Nobly spoken," said Hermes. "Impractical as hell, but that seems to go with talent. Well, I'll be here for the great fight. We're supposed to be neutral, you know, but I'll be silently cheering for Hecate. Good luck to you both."

And he flew away.

Charon had brought the ferry back, and leaped onto the shore. "I didn't expect to find you here," he said to Thallo. "I left you on this shore so you could escape, and stop nagging me. Why didn't you go?"

"For the same reason you don't. Love."

"Oh, hell," growled Charon. "All right. How do you think I can help?"

"Hearken now," said Thallo. "This Styx of yours is bottomless. Its waters grow colder and colder as they deepen, and, finally, toward earth's center, become ice. But a special kind, young sir! Black ice! A thousand times colder than the ordinary kind, and used to sheathe earth from its central fire—which, of course, is a broken-off piece of the sun."

"How do you know?" grunted Charon.

"Read it somewhere. I try to read everything written. Pick up a lot of useless knowledge that way—which sometimes comes in handy. Like now. Believe me, your river is bottomless, and grows colder as it deepens."

"Even if true, so what?"

"This is the crux of my plan, so I'll have to whisper now."

"Why?"

"I've been warned; there are spies everywhere. Flying ears, crawling eyes. Bend down, please, so you can hear me."

Charon leaned down; Thallo whispered. He went on for a long time as Charon listened, scowling. Thallo ended by saying:

"The serpents will uncoil when they're directly over the river. You'll be able to grasp their tails, and pull her down into the icy depths, deeper and deeper until she freezes stiff."

"I'll be farther down. I'll freeze stiffer."

"No, Charon. You will have kissed Persephone first. You'll be warmed by the green fire of that springtide kiss. You won't freeze."

15

The Battle, and After

The three-headed dog, Cerberus, guarded well the Gates of Hell, but it was a gloomy chore, and he quivered with eagerness now at the idea of quitting his post and fighting again. He had enrolled himself on Hecate's side. Before the coming of Charon, she had been the only one of Hades' staff to come sometimes and keep him company on his lonely vigil. Now he had become friendly with Charon also, and the ferryman had declared for Hecate, so the dog had no trouble making up his three minds about whose side he would fight on.

It was time to go. There was no one to bark at. Charon was ferrying boatload after boatload of guests across the river, and they were allowed to pass freely through the black iron gates. So the three heads of Cerberus sparred briefly with each other, warming up for the fight, then the great beast turned and trotted into Tartarus.

Preparing for his horde of guests, Hades had ordered that a vast viewing stand be erected on the Elysian Field. Here, the gods and goddesses and minor deities were to be placed according to rank. The highest seats were reserved for Zeus, Poseidon, and

Hades himself. Tactfully, he had arranged for Zeus to be seated between his brothers, and that his seat be somewhat higher.

When the guests had thronged onto the field, Thanatos, black caped and very suave, ushered them to their seats. It was a festive horde, smiling, laughing, shouting to one another. All except Hera. She didn't allow herself to frown as she moved toward her place with stately step; neither did she smile. She was furious. For she saw that a separate podium had been set aside for Zeus's beautiful daughters—his but not hers—the Muses, the Graces, and the Hours. Seated together, these radiant daughters were like a bank of flowers, and the air was murmurous with their joy.

When everyone was seated, Hades arose. Silence fell. Everyone expected him to announce the beginning of the fight. But he nodded courteously to Zeus, who arose, thanked Hades with a gracious nod, and gestured to his herald, Hermes. The herald god stood, lifted his snake-entwined staff, and called out in a silvery voice:

"Let it begin!"

The Sphinx appeared first, stalking onto the field. She was so big that one expected her to lumber like an elephant; instead she prowled like a lion. And the crowd gasped as she lifted her huge wings, tossed her mane, smiled to show her fangs, and bared her claws, batting at her own shadow. The gasping grew to cries of wonder as she spread her wings, and the huge mustard body rose into the air and hovered midway between the audience and the raftered sky.

Posed there in midair, she could be seen wholly for what she was—a winged lion larger than an elephant with claws like ivory daggers and a face too cruel to belong to any animal but the human kind—a woman's face whose black hair became a lion's mane, and whose mouth gleamed with a lion's fangs. She looked so utterly savage that Hermes, who alone among the gods had bet on Hecate, counted his wager as lost. "No one," he thought, "can possibly survive a fight with this monster of monsters."

Then, Hecate flashed into view, coming not upon the field, but floating down from the rafters, and standing on air above the artificial sun. Half-hidden as she was, she glittered among the shadows. In a nuptial verse, Thallo had described her this way:

"Her mother was a nymph of the Falcon clan, her father an eastern panther god. She looks like a cheetah partially transformed into a woman—long legged, long armed, with blazing yellow eyes. Her hands and feet are tipped with ripping claws, but, when she draws them in, her touch is as soft as velvet. Her wings are ribbed and made of membranous leather, tinged gold, wherein has arisen the report that she wears brass wings. Her followers, the Harpies, do have brass wings and brass claws and are true hags with hideous, ravaged faces. But she, their queen, is beautiful as a cheetah in midleap."

But to those gazing up at her now, she looked pathetically small compared to the Sphinx, and no one thought she had any chance at all.

Over the high seats where sat Zeus and his two brothers was stretched a canopy, and this showed foresight on the part of Hades. Soon after the fight started, it began to rain blood.

Now, the Sphinx was confident of victory, but wanted to give herself every advantage. She had strong allies and meant to use them. The strategy was to force Hecate out of the air, for she flew much faster than the Sphinx.

The Harpies were the first to attack. They had opted for the Sphinx. They expected her to become their queen in Hecate's place, and were trying to curry favor. They flew toward Hecate, separating so that they might attack from three sides. They unfurled their stingray whips as they flew. Hecate uttered a fluting call.

The audience saw things dropping out of the shadows. They

were giant snakes, friendly to Hecate. They had wound their tails about the mountain roots that were the rafters of Hell and dangled there like leather stalactites, their blunt heads weaving about Hecate.

As the Harpies flew in, shrieking, lashing, the serpents snapped their long bodies and drove their heads into the hags, smashing wings, breaking shoulder blades, knocking the Harpies out of the sky.

Drops of blood began to fall. Zeus was shielded by the canopy. The others didn't care; they were too excited by the fight to let a little blood bother them.

A pair of hundred-handed giants rushed onto the field, bearing a huge boulder in each of their two hundred hands. They hurled their rocks at Hecate. The serpents recoiled themselves and hid among the rafters. Hecate dodged the hurtling boulders, but was forced to fly lower and lower.

A squadron of dragons trotted onto the field. Wingless blue dragons, standing on their hind legs. Bred specially for the uses of Hell, they hopped swiftly, using their spiked tails for balance, and spat accurate jets of blue flame. As Hecate descended, they hopped beneath her, spitting flame, trying to incinerate her as she flew.

Then it was that Cerberus charged. He had been crouched at the end of the field, awaiting his moment. He sped for the giants, whirling about them, snarling his triple snarl. Teeth flashed, gashing a leg of each giant. But he did not stay. He flashed among the dragons. Each pair of jaws grasped a giant lizard and shook it like a rabbit. Their heads snapped; spines cracked. The broken dragons fell to the ground, spat ash, and died.

There were five dragons left, spitting flame at Cerberus. With a mighty leap he left them, landed on the grass, and stood between the dragons and the giants who were limping toward him, bellowing, and hurling boulders. Now Cerberus showed his matchless speed—dodging, weaving, leaping, charging now at the giants and slashing them until blood poured from their wounds, now leaping among the dragons and savaging them, and leaping away again.

The wounded giants kept throwing rocks, but their aim was poor now. The dragons kept spitting fire. But their flame hit the giants, and the poorly thrown rocks smashed into the dragons. The giants became lumps of charred flesh, and the dragons lay squashed—like geckos stoned by cruel boys.

Cerberus was in a battle fury; he didn't want to stop. He wrinkled three bloody maws and leaped toward the Sphinx, barking furiously. But she was too high to reach. He turned and trotted off, looking for some demons to chew on.

The crowd's attention was wrenched away from Cerberus, for Hecate and the Sphinx were closing at last. Hecate had attacked. The Sphinx was roaring; her voice rumbled like thunder as the blood drizzled down. But the blood was hers now. Hecate was darting in and out like a wasp, lashing with her stingray whip, flicking off a patch of lion hide with each blow. And the Sphinx bled. Hades watched in wonder. He had seen Hecate in action before, and had admired her, but never before had she moved as fast as she did now, and attacked with such delicate savagery. She seemed to be breaking into a swarm of hornets, each one stinging a bloody place on the beast.

But a hundred wounds didn't even begin to tap the Sphinx's enormous strength. She suffered, but she waited. Was so quiet as she hovered that she seemed almost stupefied by Hecate's attack. Again Hecate swooped, coming very close, right toward her enemy's face, trying to flick out her eyes. Too close. One great barbed paw shot out, raking Hecate from shoulder to hip.

Thallo, hiding among a fringe of myrtles at the field's edge, attached to the battle with every fiber of his being, saw his wife's tunic rip, saw claws raking bloody furrows into her flesh. Wounded, bleeding, losing strength, she was still swift. Thallo saw her rise, fly toward the rafters, the Sphinx rising in pursuit.

Up, up, flew Hecate, up to where the serpents lay coiled among the rafters. There were four serpents. She hissed at them. They obeyed instantly, two by two, twining themselves about each other. Hecate lurked in Hell's rafters, grasping a pair of braided serpents in each hand. The Sphinx hovered beneath, waiting for her to reappear.

Thallo, watching from below, watching her vanish among the shadows, knew that she had reached her last resource—which was his own plan, desperate though it was. Now he had to move. He cawed like a crow, which was his signal to Persephone, who was also hiding among the trees, keeping out of Hades' sight.

"Go!" he cried. "Run to the river as fast as you can. Kiss him once, then jump off the boat. And watch from the shore, for that's where the action will be."

She darted off, running so swiftly, so lightly, no blade of grass bent beneath her feet. Charon's ferry was moored to the near shore. He was on deck, listening to the far-off shouts of the crowd, trying to read their meaning. He saw Persephone flash through the gates, coming so fast that she was on board before he could leap ashore to greet her.

"Just time for one kiss," she whispered. "Then do what you must."

She kissed him and jumped lightly off the boat. With a mighty stroke of his oar, Charon sent the ferry to the middle of the river, and waited. He didn't have long to wait. Hecate was flying directly overhead. From each hand dangled a pair of braided snakes. The river darkened under the shadow of great wings as the Sphinx flew over.

Roaring, claws bared, she came right toward the hovering Hecate—who sank below the Sphinx and flung her snakes. They looped through the air headfirst toward the Sphinx. Four jaws clamped onto one front paw, four onto the other. They whipped their tails, trying to pull her toward the river.

They pulled her down until their tails dangled within reach

With a mighty stroke of his oar,
Charon sent the ferry to the middle
of the river, and waited.

of Charon. He stretched his arms full length and barely managed to grasp a pair of braided tails in each huge hand. He pulled. The Sphinx beat her wings and kept aloft. Charon pulled; the serpents pulled. The monster was too strong; she would not be pulled down.

Then Hecate, bleeding badly, used the very last of her strength. She forced herself to climb in the air until she was far above the Sphinx, then folded her wings like a stooping falcon and dropped with dead weight, landing on the Sphinx's broad back, between her wings.

The force of her fall combined with a final mighty yank by Charon and forced the Sphinx down, down. The monster beat her wings furiously; their downdraft capsized the ferry. Charon was thrown into the water. Quick-wittedly, he managed to clamp the ferry's anchor between his legs so that he would sink faster. Held on to the snakes as he sank, and they gripped the Sphinx. Down, down he sank, growing colder and colder. But he had kissed Persephone, drunk deeply of her springtide—and, warmed by her green fire, remembering Thallo's words, then, for love and beauty and honor and justice, he kept clenching the heavy fluke between his legs, and was dragged down, farther and farther into the freezing depths, dragging the Sphinx after him.

He felt the living cables that were the braided serpents pull out of his hands, and he knew that the Sphinx must be sinking of her own weight. He turned in the water and began to swim up—and passed the great frozen body as it sank toward the bottom.

When he surfaced, he saw that the river shore was thronged with gods and goddesses, shouting, cheering. He was disappointed. Shuddering with cold, he wanted one more kiss from Persephone to warm him again. But she was standing demurely beside Hades, and he knew that he would have to wait.

That night the guests banqueted in Hades' palace in Erebus. They reveled until dawn, then departed, thanking him for his hospitality. But the final words of Zeus were, "We're going to have to compromise, you know. Demeter is withholding her crops, and making too many people suffer, and I am being pestered by their complaints. Your bride will have to spend half a year with her mother. And that's final."

Hades had to agree, and was further dismayed when Hecate refused to serve him. She returned to Crete bearing Thallo, who dangled from her claws as they went, scribbling happily.

Nor was the Sphinx left frozen in the depth of the Styx. "Remove her," said Hades to the Cyclopes. "Take her up to the desert and deposit her in its hottest sands. It will be infernally interesting to see what happens when she thaws out in ten thousand years or so and enters a world that no longer believes in gods or monsters."

But we can't be sure that the Sphinx still languishes in the hot sands of the desert, for another legend holds that she was not frozen in the great battle but managed to escape from Tartarus and find employment with Zeus. He used her on special assign-ments—to punish those mortals who dared imitate the gods.

One such mortal was a young prince named Oedipus, who believed that he was an orphan. He came to Thebes, and in a series of accidents, killed the king—who, unbeknownst to him, happened to be his father—and married the widow—his mother— and took the Theban throne.

This angered Zeus, who did not believe in accidents and did not approve of mortals marrying their close relatives. "For," he stated, "this is a privilege reserved for the gods who must marry within the family. Take me for example: Whom could I have married without lowering myself—only my own sister."

So Zeus was displeased with Oedipus for breaking this taboo, and sent the Sphinx to kill him. Lurking in ambush beyond the city's walls, she trapped the king's chariot in a valley. She snatched up the charioteer and devoured him, armor and all, as Oedipus watched, horrified. He drew his sword to defend him-self. But the Sphinx was in no hurry; she wanted to have a little fun before killing him.

"I'll give you a chance to save your life," she said. "If you can answer this riddle, which no one has ever been able to guess, I'll let you go—or at least save you for later."

"Ask your riddle!" shouted the king.

"Very well. . . . What has sometimes two legs, sometimes three, sometimes four, and goes least when it has the most?"

"This is the answer," said Oedipus. "It is man—who walks on two legs in his prime. On three—that is, two legs and a cane— when old. And on four when a babe who can only crawl, and then goes slowest."

Now, this legend says, the Sphinx was stricken with shame at having her riddle guessed so easily—leaped off the cliff and dashed herself to pieces on the rocks below. Whereupon Zeus, still determined on punishment, sent a plague upon Thebes. And Oedipus, consulting an oracle, was told that he had brought the

The Sphinx was in no hurry;
she wanted to have a little fun
before killing him.

plague upon the city by killing his father and marrying his mother.

Then, one version of the story says, Oedipus killed himself. Another says he blinded himself. And still another that he went into exile, accompanied by his youngest daughter, who would also have been his half sister.

However, while the other tales of the Sphinx are a matter of solid record, there is very little evidence to support the Oedipus story. The account of the monster killing herself, for example, seems far out of character. Monsters value themselves too highly to commit suicide, especially this monster.

Now, Persephone did spend half of each year with her mother in the Upper World, and that time became spring and summer. Half a year she spent underground as Hades' queen. And that time, Demeter decreed, was winter, and no crops grew. As for Charon, he served as ferryman while Persephone was underground—and that was the busy season, for more old folk die in winter. And it is said that Hades by then did not care how much time Persephone spent on the ferry. For he had become interested in Menthe.

And when it was time for Persephone to visit her mother, Charon went too. He was not idle in the Upper World; he always found work as a ferryman. That he and Persephone met often then is proved by the way the most beautiful wildflowers grow on riverbanks.

We should be aware that we may not yet be finished with the Sphinx, nor she with us. There are those who say that the figure still crouching in the Egyptian desert—the figure of a monster with a lion's body, an eagle's wings, and a woman's face— is not carved out of stone but is the actual living body of the Sphinx, so deeply frozen that ninety centuries of desert sun have only begun to thaw her out. But the thawing has begun, as Hades predicted; the Sphinx is being unlocked from her frozen sleep, and will wake up hungry.

Acknowledgments

Letter Cap Illustrations by Hrana Janto

Cover, THE SPHINX *(1990) by Hrana Janto, watercolor and pastel (10 1/4" × 12")*
   Courtesy of the artist

Opposite page 1, THE SPHINX *(9th–8th century* B.C.*), Syrian bronze (5 1/4" × 5 1/8"), one of a pair*
   Courtesy of the Metropolitan Museum of Art, Rogers Fund, 1953 (53.120.1–.2)

Page 4, THE SPHINX *(1990) by Earl Staley, acrylic on canvas board (8" × 10")*
   Courtesy of the artist
     Photo: Sarah Lewis

Page 6, PACUVIUS PROCULUS, *detail from* DOUBLE PORTRAIT *(ca.* A.D. *100), fresco from Pompeii*
   Courtesy of the Museo Nazionale, Naples
     Photo: Scala/Art Resource, NY

Page 8, MOUNTAIN LANDSCAPE WITH WATERFALL *(1855) by Paul Weber, oil on canvas (40 1/4" × 34 1/4")*
   Courtesy of Christie's, NY

Page 10, *Head of* ANAVYSSOS KOUROS *(520* B.C.*), marble*
   Courtesy of the National Museum, Athens
     Photo: Art Resource, NY

Page 12, HALF FIGURE OF A MAN, NUDE TO THE WAIST *by Jean-Baptiste Deshays (1729–56), red and black chalk, heightened with white, on beige paper (11 1/5" × 12 1/7")*
   Courtesy of the Metropolitan Museum of Art, Harry G. Sperling Fund, 1985 (1985.47)

Page 14, A BATHER *by Jean-Jacques Henner (1829–1905), oil on canvas (38 1/8" × 27 3/4")*
   Courtesy of the Metropolitan Museum of Art, Bequest of Catharine Lorillard Wolfe, 1887. Catharine Lorillard Wolfe Collection (87.15.54)

Page 20, FLORA *by Arnold Böcklin (1827–1901), oil on canvas*
   Courtesy of the Museum der b. Kunste, Leipzig
     Photo: Kavaler/Art Resource, NY

Page 26, SENECA BUFFALO *or* DEVIL MASK, *painted wood with fur and leather*
   Courtesy of the Cranbrook Institute of Science, Bloomfield Hills, Michigan
     Photo: Richard Redding

Page 29, THE RAPE OF PROSERPINA *by Niccolò dell'Abate (1512–71), oil on canvas*
  Courtesy of the Louvre, Paris

Page 32, A SAILOR'S DELIGHT *by William Holbrook Beard (1825–1900), watercolor (30″ × 16 1/2″)*
  Courtesy of Christie's, NY

Page 34, NEPTUNE *by Giovanni Angelo Montorsoli (1507–63), life-size marble*
  Courtesy of the National Museum, Messina, Italy
    Photo: Scala/Art Resource, NY

Page 36, *Detail from* LANDSCAPE WITH COWS AND CAMEL *by Auguste Macke (1887–1914), watercolor*
  Courtesy of the Mostra Arte Moderna, Florence
    Photo: Art Resource, NY

Page 38, *Mask (ca. 1000), Toltec pottery from Mexico*
    Photo: The Bettmann Archive

Page 41, DEVILS WITH DANTE AND VIRGIL BY THE SIDE OF THE POOL *by William Blake (1757–1827), watercolor on paper, illustration to Dante's* DIVINE COMEDY
  Courtesy of the Tate Gallery, London
    Photo: John Webb/Art Resource, NY

Page 44, ASTARTE *by John Singer Sargent (1856–1925), oil on canvas (38 5/8″ × 12″), study for* THE PAGAN GODS, *a mural in the Boston Public Library*
  Courtesy of the Metropolitan Museum of Art, Gift of Mrs. Francis Ormond, 1950 (50.130.3)

Page 46, COUNTRY ROAD WITH ÇYPRESSES *by Giuseppe Abbati (1835–68), oil on canvas*
  Courtesy of the Modern Art Gallery, Florence
    Photo: Scala/Art Resource, NY

Page 48, *Head of kouros (520 B.C.), marble*
  Courtesy of the National Museum, Athens
    Photo: Art Resource, NY

Page 50, SPHINX *(ca. 450–425 B.C.), Greek sculptured gravestone, crowning member, marble*
  Courtesy of the Metropolitan Museum of Art, Munsey Fund, 1936, 1938; Hewitt Fund, 1911 (11.185 cd)

Page 54, TOUCHES OF SUN ON THE TERRACE *by Maurice Denis (1870–1943), oil on canvas*
  Courtesy of a private collection
    Photo: Art Resource, copyright 1990 ARS, NY/SPADEM

Page 57, CAT AND I *by Wanda Wultz (1903–84), gelatin silver print (11 9/16″ × 9 1/4″)*
  Courtesy of the Metropolitan Museum of Art, Gift of Ford Motor Company and John C. Waddell, 1987 (1987.1100.123)

Page 58, MOUNTAIN LANDSCAPE *by C. D. Friedrich (1774–1840), oil on canvas*
  Courtesy of the Neue Pinakothek, Munich
    Photo: Kavaler/Art Resource, NY

BOOKS BY BERNARD EVSLIN

Merchants of Venus
Heroes, Gods and Monsters of the Greek Myths
Greeks Bearing Gifts: The Epics of Achilles and Ulysses
The Dolphin Rider
Gods, Demigods and Demons
The Green Hero
Heraclea
Signs & Wonders: Tales of the Old Testament